Nazi propaganda in one battle, on a single day
Cassino, Italy, May 11, 1944

PAPER WAR

Nazi propaganda in one battle, on a single day
Cassino, Italy, May 11, 1944

With an Introduction by
Randall L. Bytwerk

Mark Batty Publisher

Thursday, May 11, 1944

This book contains German propaganda fired at the 8th Indian Division of 13 British Corps during a single day: Thursday, May 11, 1944. I was a liaison officer attached to the 8th Indian Division and took part in the action that occurred later that night. This was the first day of the fourth battle of Monte Cassino, which started at 11 pm. Earlier in the day the Germans had fired propaganda leaflets at us, and I made a collection of them which I kept in my knapsack. This book reproduces the leaflets that I picked up that day.

Thursday, May 11, 1944, was warm but dull and there was some light rain. Visibility was good in the morning but in the afternoon, fog rolled into the Rapido Valley and helped to contribute to a false sense of relative calm throughout most of that day. We spent our time getting ready for the offensive planned for that night; checking and rechecking all the details.

It is hard to convey the intensity of the battle that had been raging since January. A little calm would have been quite welcome except that we knew that we would be involved in an important and powerful offensive at the end of the day. Waiting is hard when you know that a major and dangerous battle, with inevitably heavy casualties, is just a few hours away. We had planned to reduce artillery fire during the afternoon and to come to a standstill in the early evening to accentuate the idea of our disinterest, and in this way to maximize the outcome of the offensive. What we had not expected was that the Germans would also cease fire at roughly the same time as we did, and this had the consequence of creating an unnatural quiet the likes of which we had not experienced for months. This quiet was sinister and oppressive, and after a couple of hours, had to be broken by sporadic and random bursts of Allied fire that gave a sense of normality to both sides.

At 11 pm a powerful bombardment along the entire 18-mile German line, which stretched from the coast to the upper Rapido valley, started with a roar. It was a pitch-dark night, doubtless enhanced by the mist, although there was a late moon and some stars that provided reasonable visibility. The intense noise of shellfire was further dramatized by many bright and enduring patches of light caused by shells exploding and targets burning.

The offensive against the Germans was international: British, American, French, Indian, Moroccan, and Polish troops were all part of the effort. The Allied attempt involved the mountain fighters of several Moroccan Divisions and the US II Corps in an offensive on Monte Faito in the Aurunci mountains, not far from the coast. Four French divisions made substantial inroads to the north of the Moroccans and the Americans.

Just after the French got going, we set out to the right of them in our assault boats on the Rapido River to the south of Cassino and the bridge on Route 6. We made good headway and successfully crossed the river. Then the Polish II Corps went into attack and advanced on Widmo and Monte Calvario: their losses were heavy and they fought with tremendous courage.

The battle continued into the next day and concentrated fighting renewed the following night, and it was not until the early morning of May 18 that the Germans finally retreated and some Polish soldiers were the first to climb over the walls of the ruined Abbey of Monte Cassino.

Before the battle started during the night of May 11, the Germans had been firing propaganda leaflets at the soldiers of the 8th Indian Division of 13 British Corps. This paper bombardment had been going on all day. We were waiting for the offensive to begin near the bank of the Rapido River below Monte Cassino, more or less on the German Gustav line and about two-thirds of the way up, and the leaflets just kept coming.

At first the Germans thought we were a British Divi-

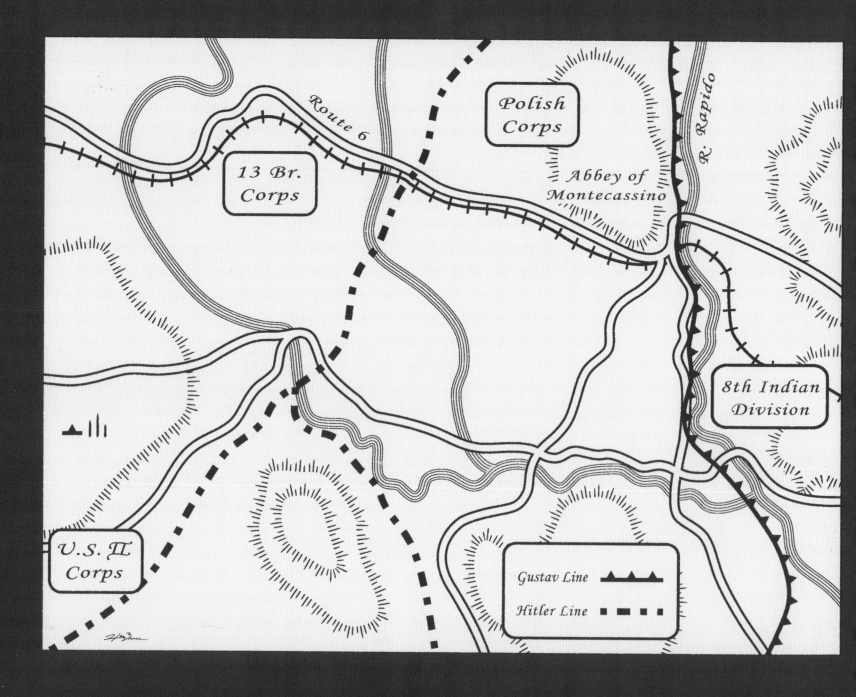

6

Route 6

Polish
Corps

13 Br.
Corps

Abbey of
Montecassino

R. Rapido

8th Indian
Division

U.S. II
Corps

Gustav Line

Hitler Line

This map shows the deployment of international forces at the beginning
of the Fourth Battle of Monte Cassino, on May 11-12, 1944.

sion and fired two pieces of propaganda at us in English (leaflets 1 and 2).

The Poles, who were on our right, were quickly identified, and the Germans then thought for a while that we were part of the Polish forces. It seemed they held this view for several hours during which they fired nine different examples of propaganda in Polish (leaflets 3 to 11). We were finally recognized as Indian, and the next three examples of propaganda (leaflets 12 to 14) are in Urdu and Hindi.

All fourteen of these propaganda pieces were fired by mortar from a launcher positioned on the Cassino side of the Rapido River, which we captured a few days after we crossed over. At the time I made some sketches and notes of the launcher in my notebook.

The Allies responded to the German propaganda effort with their own propaganda barrage: a safe conduct (leaflet 15) and a contemptuous "Wo ist Hitler?" (leaflet 16), "Where is Hitler?", because Hitler, the leader, had not been seen in public for many months by that point, providing opportunity for propaganda speculation.

The output of the German propaganda printing presses having been so heavy that day, the Allied High Commander deemed it advisable to circulate among us—with a translation—an example of its own efforts (leaflets 17 and 18), a letter from a German girl to her soldier sweetheart.

The final piece in the book is Field Marshall Alexander's Special Order of the Day (leaflet 19), published one year after the battle of Cassino, announcing victory in Italy. I have included it because for me, it represents closure to the events of that day.

In spite of the volume of propaganda material fired at us on that Thursday in May, the effect that it had on us was considerably less dramatic than those minutes of total silence that we had experienced earlier in the afternoon of the 11th. Propaganda in the heat of battle can of course demoralize, but only in conjunction with other events. The events I have described took place and are now silent history, real only to those of us who were there. Not so with printed propaganda: we still have these to look at, and they help to give a sense of the horror of war, and just a glimpse of how it was on that mountain on that day.

Peter Batty

This spread shows the sketches and notes made by Peter Batty during the Battle of Cassino. The drawings explain the captured mortar launcher that had been used to scatter the propaganda leaflets featured in this book.

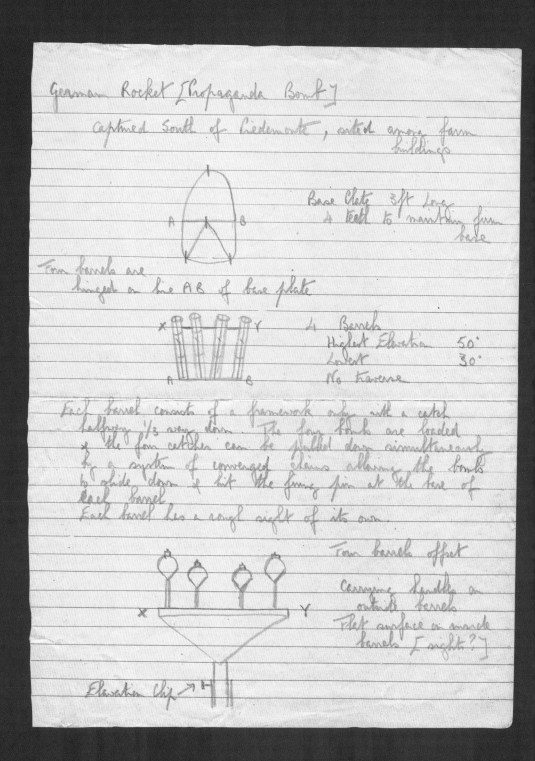

Section through barrel

Framework

Solid triangular base   Catch & Pull Chain

Bomb — Three screw portions
1. Detonator
2. Explosive
3. Propaganda Case

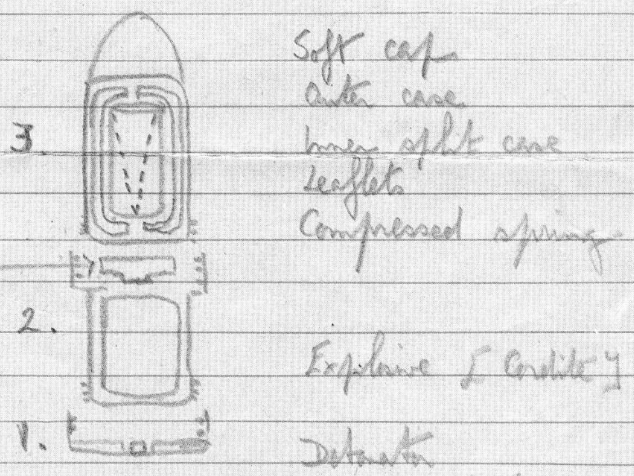

3.   Soft cap
                     Outer case
                     Inner split case
                     Leaflets
                     Compressed spring

Smaller charge ————

[This charge is just sufficient   2.
to blow soft cap off, thus
pushing out the leaflets   Explosive [Cordite]
which are scattered by the
compressed spring.]   1.   Detonator

9

WORDS AT WAR
Randall L. Bytwerk

Making propaganda is not as easy as it looks. People see film clips of Hitler at the Nuremberg rallies, of huge Nazi mass marches, and conclude that Germans blindly followed their leaders, victims of irresistible propaganda. That is not what the Nazis thought. To them, propaganda was serious business, hard work. As Hitler wrote in *Mein Kampf*, propaganda is effective "only after a sometimes unbelievably tough and thorough belaboring of soul and mind." And that is when one is attempting to persuade one's own country. It is far harder to persuade the enemy, someone unwilling to grant the premises that support an argument. As Francis Cornford once said in jest, propaganda can be the art of "very nearly deceiving one's friends without quite deceiving one's enemies."

This book provides examples of propaganda aimed at the enemy: leaflets that showered on Allied and German troops in Italy before the fourth and final assault on Cassino that began on May 11, 1944. They are vivid pieces of interesting propaganda.

Joseph Goebbels claimed that the Third Reich was made by propaganda, and he knew what he was talking about. The rise of Hitler's movement from a tiny group meeting in the back room of a Munich pub in 1919 to the mass movement that took over the state in 1933 is a case study of effective propaganda. The Nazis put enormous effort into making propaganda, and made so much of it that they overwhelmed the other German political parties. For example, the Nazis held hundreds of thousands of public meetings before 1933, sometimes holding more meetings in an area than all other parties combined (there were over 30!). They pioneered the use of radio, aerial travel, and film in political propaganda. Their posters and speeches were vivid, hard to ignore.

In all they did, both before and after 1933, the Nazis followed the guidelines Hitler provided in *Mein Kampf*, written in 1924 and 1925. The book is long and often

turgid, but when he turns to propaganda, Hitler is clear. In two chapters centering on propaganda, and in passing comments throughout the book, he told the Nazis what they had to do to persuade the masses. In brief, propaganda had to be simple, put in terms that "even the last member of the public will understand." It should be repeated constantly, though not in exactly the same way. It needed to be one-sided. What would you think, Hitler asks, of a soap company whose advertising did not claim it had the best soap? "All advertising, whether in the field of business or politics, achieves success through the continuity and sustained uniformity of its application." Propaganda should not be different. And propaganda should appeal to the emotions. Hitler did not avoid reasoning, and in fact could build a persuasive, well-argued, and supported case when he wanted to. But as he put it in *Mein Kampf*: "The art of propaganda lies in understanding the emotional ideas of the great masses and finding, through a psychologically correct form, the way to the attention and thence to the heart of the broad masses." For Hitler, there was one standard for judging propaganda: effectiveness. If it achieved the desired result, it was good. Other criteria were irrelevant.

Joseph Goebbels was a brilliant tactician of propaganda, but he had little to say about strategy that Hitler had not said already. People often imagine Nazi Germany as one organized, carefully coordinated system. Goebbels, they think, who was appointed Minister for People's Enlightenment and Propaganda in March 1933, controlled the vast apparatus of propaganda, which fell upon the Germans in a uniform deluge. The truth is more complicated. Although Goebbels was the central propaganda figure in the Third Reich, he had competition on every side. Hitler granted his subordinates overlapping areas of responsibility, so leading Nazis were always watching their competitors warily, jealously guarding their power. Goebbels shared control of the press, the arts, publishing, foreign propaganda, and mass meetings, for example. He constantly complained about other Nazi leaders who, to his thinking, tried to make propaganda without knowing much about it.

There is a tendency to equate propaganda with lying, something neither Hitler nor Goebbels agreed with. Both wanted propaganda to be as truthful as possible (although both were willing to lie boldly when necessary). Lying is, after all, dangerous. It can be found out. It is much better to mislead by selecting, omitting, or downplaying facts. That also is a form of lying (two half truths do not make one whole truth), but is harder for the enemy to exploit.

Goebbels had limited influence over German military propaganda. Civilian and military propagandists did not always talk with each other. For example, Goebbels had created propaganda proclaiming the sinking of the British aircraft carrier *Ark Royal* in 1940. When he later complained to the navy that it was still afloat, their dry response was that it had been sunk by the Propaganda Ministry, not by them.

That brings us to this collection of leaflets, which Goebbels would not have seen. That does not mean they followed different principles of propaganda. Both the military and civilian branches used the same basic propaganda tactics, with varying degrees of skill.

The Germans and the Allies had propaganda (or psychological warfare) teams attached to combat units in the field. Little is known of what happened in Italy on the German side, since the records were destroyed. We do know the Germans were active. The collector's catalog of German leaflets during the Italian campaign lists over 780 leaflets directed toward Allied troops. The examples in this book are a small but reasonably representative sample of the paper that Allied troops encountered. German leaflets were generally delivered by

artillery shells. Some were scattered by soldiers in the hope that they would blow over to the enemy side, or be picked up as the enemy advanced.

The Allies had more resources. They dropped seven million leaflets before the invasion of Sicily in July 1943, for example, something beyond German capacities. Using artillery shells and aircraft, they delivered several million copies each week of the *Frontpost*, a leaflet-style newspaper, to Germans on the Italian front. During the Cassino campaign, the Allies used a large printing press capable of printing eight thousand leaflets an hour. It was hauled around by a captured German tank carrier.

The town of Cassino blocked the path to Rome, less than a hundred miles north, for five months. It was surrounded by grim mountains. The valleys were narrow, reducing the advantage of the Allied superiority in equipment and numbers. The Allies tried major offensives in January, February, and March 1944, but were unable to break through. Allied forces landed at Anzio on January 22, between Cassino and Rome, but the Germans were able to contain the beachhead. In May 1944, the front was a stalemate.

The ancient monastery of St. Benedict, towering fifteen hundred feet above the valley, was bombed in February. The ruins of its twenty-foot thick walls provided an almost impregnable position for the Germans, who occupied it only after it had been reduced to imposing rubble. It is hard to imagine a better defensive position. The fighting at Cassino was among the toughest of the war. Some Germans who had fought at Stalingrad thought that Cassino was the harder battle. In the first three battles, the brunt was carried by American, British, French North African, and New Zealand troops. The fourth battle drew in Indian and Polish units as well.

On May 11, the Allies launched a final and successful offensive. Polish troops led the attack on the monastery, while other troops fought through and past the city. This

A view of the Abbey on Monastery Hill, Cassino, May 19, 1944 (Courtesy of the Imperial War Museum).

time, the Allies carried the day. By May 19, the town and the monastery had been captured and the Germans had withdrawn to their next positions.

Before the battle, the Germans showered Allied positions outside the town of Cassino with leaflets in a variety of languages, since they were not always sure of whom they were facing. On a single day, the Germans dropped the leaflets in this book on Allied troops near Monte Cassino in English, Polish, Hindi, and Urdu.

Making propaganda to the enemy is particularly challenging. Allied troops reading German leaflets (assuming they could read the language!) had good reason to doubt that the Germans had their best interests at heart — perhaps the Poles above all. They had been the first victims of the war and had no cause to trust German promises. Although many Indians favored independence from the British, and the Nazis supported various schemes to encourage Indian resistance to British rule, most Indian troops were loyal to the Crown.

Propaganda aimed at the enemy usually has relatively modest goals, which sometimes made soldiers doubt their worth. Allied pilots, for example, complained about risking their lives to drop leaflets instead of bombs, with the result that they were given English translations of the German-language leaflets to persuade them that words could be weapons too. A classic Bill Mauldin cartoon showed American soldiers firing artillery at the Germans. One says: "Tell them leaflet people th' krauts ain't got time fer readin' today." Their sentiments changed as they saw Germans surrender.

Leaflets have useful results. They do not win battles, but they can reduce morale. Demoralized soldiers do not fight well. A few soldiers will desert to the enemy side. Others choose to disappear behind the lines (relatively easy in Italy), to surrender rather than fight to the death in a tight position, or to pretend illness to escape the front lines. This was a problem for both sides. The

Nazis executed 50,000 of their own soldiers for desertion or cowardice during World War II. The Americans convicted 21,000 soldiers of desertion, though only one was executed. The number who faked illness (or literally shot themselves in the foot) is harder to estimate. Any of these alternatives was useful to the opposing side. An enemy removed, whether by military action or propaganda, is one less enemy to fight.

These leaflets focus on three topics: loved ones back home, personal survival, and news. There was little chance of making Nazis of Allied troops or democrats of Germans, and neither side tried. Instead, they concentrated on the universal concerns of men facing violent death under miserable conditions. Enemy leaflets provided reading material, always in short supply at the front. They further served a useful purpose as toilet paper — often scarce.

Most of the leaflets in this collection deal with those at home. Leaflet 2, intended for British troops, exploited frictions within the Allied coalition. It was one of several similar German leaflets used in the Italian campaign. There were hundreds of thousands of American G.I.s in England, preparing for the Normandy invasion, and they were well paid by British standards. As envious Brits put it, the problem with the Americans was that they were "overpaid, oversexed, and over here." British soldiers in Italy could see that the Americans had seemingly inexhaustible supplies, better food, and more money. The leaflet tells an amusing story calculated to arouse jealousy. The Germans had directed the same argument, by the way, to French soldiers on the Maginot Line in 1939-1940, except that French soldiers were told it was British troops who were enjoying romance in Paris while they faced the Germans.

Leaflets aimed at the Poles raised graver threats than that of free-spending Yanks. As the battle commenced, the Red Army was driving the Nazis back into pre-war Poland. The Poles hardly loved the Germans, but most of the Polish force in Italy had bitter experience with the Soviets, too. They had been hauled by the Russians to labor camps, where they spent four years before an Allied agreement brought them through Iran to North Africa for training. These refugee soldiers feared what would happen to their families coming under Soviet rule, which the Germans tried to exploit. Leaflet 3, for example, has "Go Home!" under a picture of a child. "Your children are in grave danger," it begins. Leaflets 4-11 all mention in one way or another the threat to families in Poland. The Soviets were entering Poland, and who knew what they would do. These leaflets were likely unsettling.

The Nazis hit real concerns in these leaflets, particularly when mentioning Katyn. This was the forest in eastern Poland, discovered the year before, where the Soviets had murdered about 4,000 Polish officers in 1939. The Nazis exaggerated the figure (leaflet 7 claims 12,000 dead), but Katyn was a welcome topic for Nazi propaganda. The Soviets denied the massacre, but the Germans invited in the International Red Cross, which agreed that the Soviets had been responsible. This put the Western Allies in an unpleasant situation. They had agreed that Stalin could keep the Polish territory he had conquered in 1939, and did not want to risk a major break with Stalin, since 80% of the German army was in the East. There was no way to deny the allegations, so they did their best to ignore it. However, despite the understandable concerns, the Poles fought with courage and sacrifice.

The leaflets aimed at colonial Indian troops use a similar argument. Why are Indian troops fighting for their masters when revolution is going on at home? Leaflet 12 tells a story that encourages Indians to fight for independence, not for their British rulers in Italy. Leaflet 13 notes that the Japanese and Germans were supporting Subhash Chandra Bose, a leader in the Indian independence movement. He spent six months in Berlin in 1941 in a not particularly successful effort to win German support before moving to Japan to encourage military action. The leaflets commend the valor of enemy soldiers while suggesting that Poles and Indians were fighting for a bad cause. Psychologically, this makes good sense, since suggesting that enemy soldiers are cowards will stiffen rather than reduce their willingness to fight.

The second common theme was safety. These leaflets deal with it in a variety of ways. Leaflet 1 presents sunny Italy and a bathing beauty on one side (pin-up girls were a standard theme in leaflets), death on the other. Leaflets 4 and 5 have vivid drawings of soldiers dying in battle. Leaflet 9 is a purported letter from a Polish deserter to the German side, who reports that he is being treated well, and will soon be able to go home. Leaflet 10 encourages desertion by providing news of several Polish deserters, and encouraging readers to listen to a German shortwave station for more information. The problem with the latter leaflets is that deserting to the losing side is not attractive — and it was clear that the Germans were losing the war, even if slowly.

A standard argument in the leaflets was that the soldiers in the front lines were brave dupes. Whether it was British soldiers whose girlfriends were being seduced by Americans back home, or Polish troops dying for England while being sold out to the Russians, or Indian troops bleeding for their colonial masters, the point was that soldiers were fighting for something other than their best interests.

Persuading soldiers to desert is a delicate business. For example, the American army first planned to use leaflets aimed at German soldiers in Italy that promised good treatment at prisoner of war camps in North America, including eggs for breakfast. Although that was in fact the case, when the leaflets were tested on captured German soldiers in Italy, they simply refused to believe it. Even though they were receiving better treatment than they expected in POW camps, it was beyond their ability to believe that the Allies would actually feed prisoners fresh eggs. New leaflets promising fair, but rigorous, treatment were hurriedly prepared. Leaflet 15 is along these lines. It simply promises Germans decent care and removal to safety. The German leaflets to Poles make the unlikely promise that they will be sent directly home to see how their loved ones were doing.

The final leaflet theme was news. Soldiers at the front eagerly got whatever information they could, whether from friend of foe, and rumors spread readily. No leaflet "newspapers" are included in this group. However, leaflet 10 encourages Polish soldiers to listen to Radio Wanda, a German radio transmitter aimed at Polish troops. Allied leaflet 16, which asks "Where is Hitler?" on one side, and proclaims "Heil Himmler" on the other, exploits the fact that Hitler rarely appeared in public during this stage of the war. Germans had last heard his voice on January 30, 1944, the anniversary of the Nazi takeover in 1933. Internal German public opinion reports found that people longed to hear him speak, and worried when he was silent for a long period. Soldiers did not trust the enemy's portrayal of events, but these leaflets were read, and surely had an impact. They built on fear and uncertainty.

Some aspects of Nazi ideology did show up in leaflets, particularly anti-Semitism, which the Germans persisted in believing that the Allied side was almost ready to accept. The best example in this file is leaflet 8, which shows a comely naked lass in the arms of an ugly Jew. There was a long Polish anti-Semitic tradition. Since Nazi anti-Semitism was well known, the Jew shown presumably is in London or New York rather than occupied Poland, making his fortune from Polish blood. Leaflet 11 plays the racist card by telling the Poles that they were being treated even worse than colonial colored troops.

However, ideological leaflets were far less common than leaflets on home, safety, or news. Both sides usually realized they were ineffective.

The leaflets in this book were read in 1944 by men who might die at any moment. Although propaganda did not decide the battle, it was a significant factor in influencing morale, that hard to define characteristic that helps soldiers decide whether to keep fighting even at the risk of death, or act in a way likely to keep them alive. As an American psychological warfare officer told a general during World War II: "You see, General, it works something like this: you and your men push the krauts to the edge of the precipice and then we come along and push them over." These leaflets may not have pushed many soldiers on the other side over the precipice, but even small effects influence battles.

For more information:

Herz, Martin F. "Some Psychological Lessons from Leaflet Propaganda in World War II," Public Opinion Quarterly 13 (1949), 471-486. Herz was in charge of leaflet writing for the American Fifth Army during the Cassino campaign.

Herzstein, Robert E. The War That Hitler Won: The Most Infamous Propaganda Campaign in History (New York: G. P. Putnam's Sons, 1978). A good book on Nazi propaganda during the war.

Margolin, Leo J. Paper Bullets: A Brief Story of Psychological Warfare in World War II (New York: Froben Press, 1946). Margolin was a news editor attached to the American Psychological Warfare Branch during World War II.

Parker, Matthew. Monte Cassino: The Hardest-Fought Battle of World War II (New York: Doubleday, 2004). The best book on the battles at Cassino.

Internet sites:

German Propaganda Archive (http://www.calvin.edu/cas/gpa/): A wide collection of German propaganda translated into English, including some leaflets dropped at Normandy.

The Psywar Society (http://www.psywarsoc.org/): The international society of collectors interested in military leaflets and psychological warfare.

their power. Goebbels shared control of the press, the arts, publishing, foreign propaganda, and mass meetings, for example. He constantly complained about other Nazi leaders who, to his thinking, tried to make propaganda without knowing much about it.

There is a tendency to equate propaganda with lying, something neither Hitler nor Goebbels agreed with. Both wanted propaganda to be as truthful as possible (although both were willing to lie boldly when necessary). Lying is, after all, dangerous. It can be found out.

The following two spreads show a reproduction of an article from the German magazine, *Illustrierter Beobachter*. The topic of this article is the bravery of the German soldiers at Monte Cassino. The article is shown as it was originally, followed by a translation spread.

18

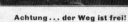

Der Aufstieg in die Bergstellungen der Cassino-Front

Eine Fallschirmjägerkampfgruppe zieht mit Waffen, Gerät und Sturmgepäck beladen den mühevollen, steinigen Pfad nach oben. Vier Stunden dauert dieser Anstieg.

Überraschung für die Angreifer

In den Trümmern des zerstörten Klosters, das jetzt in unsere Hauptkampflinie miteinbezogen wurde, haben sich die kleinen, aber kampfkräftigen Trupps unserer Fallschirmjäger festgesetzt

Achtung . . . der Weg ist frei!

Das zerstörte Kloster Monte Cassino erhält mit uhrwerkartiger das Störungsfeuer der britischen Artillerie. Der Melder wartet ab. Klatschend fahren die Granatsplitter und Steinbrocken geg Jetzt ist der Weg frei zum Gefechtsstand der Fallschirmjäge überquert der Melder den gefährdeten Raum.

DIE HELDEN VON MONTE CASSI

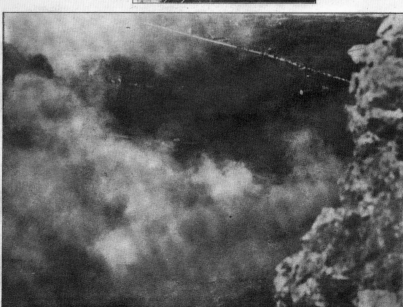

Ungeahnte Kunstschät

fielen den Terrorbombern zum fer. Nur ein kleines Beispiel: T des Benedikt.

Rollendes Artilleriefeuer de Briten und Amerikaner liegt dem Cassino-Massiv und i Cassino-Tal.

Das schluchtenreiche, von Höhlen du furchte Gelände bietet unseren Fallsch jägern Deckung und Sicherheit.

Links:
Oberst Heilmann
der Kommandeur eines Fallschirmjäger-Regimentes, das die Trümmerstätte von Cassino heldenhaft verteidigt, wurde vom Führer mit dem Eichenlaub zum Ritterkreuz des Eisernen Kreuzes ausgezeichnet.

Wie Katzen
geschmeidig in die zackigen Brocken des zerrissenen Gesteins eingeschmiegt, fangen unsere Fallschirmjäger die immer von neuem vorgetragenen Angriffe der Anglo-Amerikaner auf.

Links:
Trotz Bomben und Granaten
Unerschütterlich sind unsre Tapferen.

PK.-Aufnahmen:
Kriegsberichter Beuschel (4),
Czirnich (3), Schneiders (1),
Dr. Stocker (1).

Solch eine Brücke
hält schwerstes Trommeln aus. Nur manchmal gibt's nasse Füße

The Heroes of Monte Cassino
Illustrierter Beobachter, 13 April 1944, pp. 2-3.

Captions of the pictures:

1. **Climbing to mountain fortifications on the Cassino front**
A company of paratroopers, with weapons, equipment, and packs, on the rocky, wearying path upwards. The climb takes four hours.

2. **A surprise for the attackers**
In the ruins of the monastery, now on the front line, the small but battle-tested detachment of our paratroopers has established its position.

3. **Attention! The way is open!**
With clockwork regularity, British artillery fires on the ruins of the monastery of Monte Cassino. A messenger waits out the attack. Shell splinters and rocks pound against the walls. Now the way to the paratrooper positions is free. The messenger dashes across the treacherous open area.

4. **Countless art treasures**
were destroyed by terror bombing. A single small example: a torso of St. Benedict.

5. **Rolling American and British artillery fire over Mt. Cassino and the Cassino valley**
The hilly area, with its many narrow canyons and caves, offers our paratroopers cover and safety.

1.

2.

3.

4.

5.

6. Colonel Heilmann
The Führer awarded the Knight's Cross with oak leaves to the commander of a paratroop regiment that is heroically defending the ruins of Cassino.

7. Like cats
our paratroopers find cover in ragged piles of fallen stones from the steady Anglo-American attacks.

8. Despite bombs and shells
our brave men are unshakable.

9. Such an arch
withstands the heaviest barrage. Occasionally, however, feet get wet.

The *Illustrierter Beobachter* was the illustrated weekly of the Nazi Party.

6.

7.

8.

9.

PROPAGANDA LEAFLETS

ITALY

wants to see you

But did you expect to find it like this?

Leaflet 1 back

Before attempting the break through at Cassino, your command withdrew all American troops from the main fighting line, because — as was stated by the B. B. C. on 23. 3. 44 — only picked allied troops could be used against the German parachutists.

It is not our intent at this moment to talk about the brave New Zealanders and Indians who have not succeeded either — for the simple reason that the German troops turned out to be even tougher and braver. But it is worth while thinking over why London has such a bad opinion about your American pals.

Possibly, because 70% of all Americans who came across are still hanging about in England?

Possibly, because the moral in England has reached such a deplorably low level, thanks to the "American liberties"?

Possibly, because no girl and no woman in England is feeling safe of the snares that are constantly being laid by the American officers and soldiers?

Yet, not all of them have the presence of mind displayed by the young lady about whom Mrs. Eileen Jones of Cardiff told her husband, Sgt. G. H. Jones, "C" Squadron 40th B. R. T. R., C. M. F. No. 1917551. In one of her letters she wrote:

This is a story Grace heard.

An American officer had been friendly with a group of young women and he was known to ask for what he wanted because he knew he was able to pay for his enjoyment. One night he was out with a young woman to whom he showed a wallet containing Ł 46. He posed a certain question to which she answered yes — if he'd remove his trousers first!! He must have been a trusting soul — for she grabbed his trousers and ran off. According to the version heard by Grace he was wandering round the streets looking for cover! I hardly know whether to believe this or not — but I suppose it could be true. —

Now, even if this story should be exaggerated, it shows nevertheless that the "training" of the American soldiers in England is making progress. Not too pleasant for a poor English ground hog who is thinking of his girl or his wife at home!

But this is the fact — while you are stuck in the mud they are waging an amusing war in England. Therefore they are also being paid about twice as much as you are — so that they should be able to wave filled wallets in case their charm alone would not be inducing enough.

LWP 125/4-44

Leaflet 2 back

28

GO HOME!

Kolego Polaku!

Twoje dzieci znajdują się w obliczu niebezpieczeństwa! Walczysz w szeregach sprzymierzeńców bolszewików, którzy wtargnęli na wschodnie kresy Polski, na ziemie ojczyste, aby obrócić je w perzynę i zamienić na jedno wielkie cmentarzysko.

Pomyśl zatem o Twoich dzieciach którym obecnie zagraża straszne niebezpieczeństwo! W obliczu niebezpieczeństwa czerwonej nawały, grożącej zarówno Tobie jak i wszystkim kulturalnym narodom europejskim, żołnierz niemiecki podaje Ci rękę i na rozkaz Adolfa Hitlera zapewnia Ci natychmiastowe zwolnienie i powrót do Ojczyzny, jeśli przybędziesz bez broni do nas.

Twoim hasłem są słowa „Do domu!" Niemieckie posterunki oczekują Cię i pozwolą Ci dostać się w bezpieczne miejsce.

Pamiętaj o Twoich dzieciach!

S. 419.

DEAR POLISH FRIEND!

Your children are in grave danger. You are fighting in the ranks of the Allied Bolsheviks, who have invaded your Fatherland from the East to change it into a burial-ground.

So think of your children who, in particular, are facing terrible danger. In the face of this danger, which is threatening you and all other cultural European countries, the German soldier is offering you a hand, and on Adolf Hitler's command, assures you instant dismissal if you surrender to us.

Your slogan is "Go Home!". The German posts are awaiting you and will help you reach a safe place.

Remember your children!

POLISH FRIEND

DO YOU WANT
TO DIE HERE?

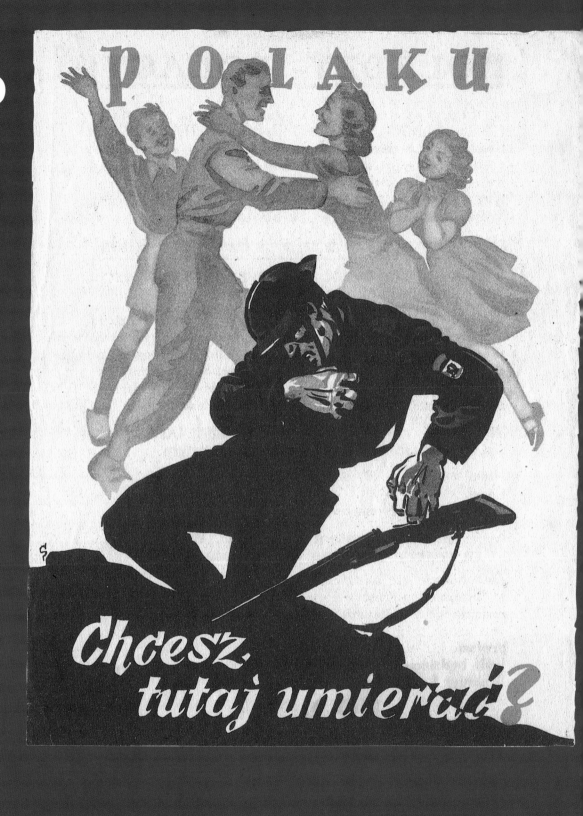

KOLEDZY- POLACY!

Wielu z Was napewno zna strzelca Jana Lubczyńskiego z 2 kompanji, 3 Bataljonu, 1 Brygady, 3 Dywizji Wojsk Polskich. Nie jest wykluczone, że niejeden z Was jechał z nim transportem do Borespola, lub poźniej służył z nim w Palestynie. Niezawodnie wiecie o tem, że Janek jest dobrym kolegą, że jest dobrym synem Ojczyzny Polski i że nie trwożą go okrucieństwa wojny.

Kolega Lubczyński przybył do nas w ub. Poniedziałek Wielkanocny.

Troska o przyszłość Ojczyzny oraz szczęście rodziny skłoniły go do powrotu do domu.

Wychodzi on z założenia, że udział w walkach na ziemi włoskiej niema żadnego sensu. Strzelec Lubczyński zdaje sobie sprawę z potwornego widma śmierci i zgrozy nadciągającej ze wschodu w postaci czerwonych armij, zagrażających jego rodzinie i dlatego w chwili największego niebezpieczeństwa pragnie być podporą matki.

W Ciągu najbliższych 14 dni Jan Lubczyński znajdzie się w domu rodzinnym.

Prosi, by Was pozdrowić. Obecnie wiedzie się mu dobrze i jest dobrej myśli. Wszystko, co ma na sercu i co spotkało go u Niemców » Sam Wam opowie. «

Słuchajcie zatem rozgłośni „ Wanda " a usłyszycie kolegę Jana Lubczyńskiego!

Zastanówcie się nad tem, czy wolicie polec we Włoszech za Stalina i sowiecką Polskę, czy też udać się do domu rodzinnego z zapewnieniem Adolfa Hitlera, że będziecie tam mogli żyć w otoczeniu rodziny, oczekując lepszej przyszłości Waszej ukochanej Ojczyzny.
Jeśli będziecie przechodzili do nas, nie zapominajcie, że Waszym hasłem jest

DO DOMU!

S 414

DEAR POLISH FRIENDS!

Many of you probably know the shooter Jan Lubczynski from 2 Company, 3 Battalion, 1 Brigade, 3 Polish Army Division. Many of you probably went with him by transport to Borespola, and later served with him in Palestine. You probably know that Jan is a good friend, is loyal to his Fatherland, and that he's not worried by the cruelties of the war.

JAN LUBCZYNSKI CAME TO US ON EASTER MONDAY. ANXIETY OVER POLAND'S FUTURE AND HIS FAMILY'S HAPPINESS MADE HIM RETURN HOME.

His principle is that there's no point in taking part in battles on Italian ground. The shooter Lubczynski realizes the impending death and horrors approaching from the East in the form of the Red Army, threatening his family and he wishes to be able to comfort his mother in this moment of great danger.

IN THE NEXT 14 DAYS, JAN LUBCZYNSKI WILL FIND HIMSELF AT HOME

He's asked us to send you his regards. Things are going well for him and he's in good spirit. He'll tell you himself his opinion of the Germans and how he's been treated.

SO LISTEN TO THE "WANDA" BROADCAST TO HEAR YOUR FRIEND JAN LUBCZYNSKI.

Consider if you'd prefer to be killed in Italy for Stalin and Soviet Poland, or go home to your family with Hitler's assurance that you, and your family, can expect a better future in your beloved Fatherland.
If you do come to us, remember your slogan is:

GO HOME!

POLISH FRIENDS

GO TO

CASSINO!

Żołnierze Polscy!

Grozi Wam wielkie niebezpieczeństwo. Ominął Was Katyń, uszliście z życiem z raju bolszewickiego. Mieliście dotychczas szczęście - - - ale teraz jesteście niepożądani. Zespolone formacje polskie nie podobają się Stalinowi, który dąży do zniszczenia Waszej Ojczyzny. Wasi wodzowie w Londynie otrzymali z Moskwy instrukcje zlikwidowania Was w sposób nieskomplikowany.

Przebywaliście narazie na spokojnych pozycjach środkowego odcinku frontu włoskiego. Teraz macie być rzuceni w piekło Cassina. Przed kilku laty Stalin wysłał ekipę morderców aby zlikwidowała w Katyniu kolegów Waszych. Ale anglicy są sprytniejsi. Wysyłają Was na front Cassino, abyście mogli polec w aueroli bohaterstwa.

Polscy żołnierze!

Czy orjętujecie się w tej grze, w którą Was wciągnięto?

W tej sytuacji pozostała Wam tylko jedna deska ratunku - przejście do nas a znowu ujrzycie Ojczyznę. Pod ochroną niemieckich żołnierzy, którzy piersią osłaniają Europę, a tym samym Polskę przed nawałą bolszewicką, będziecie mogli spokojnie pracować według własnej woli i upodobania.

Dwa słowa

DO DOMU!

zadecydują o przyszłości Waszej, o życiu lub śmierci.

Podajcie to hasło pierwszemu napodkanemu na froncie żołnierzowi niemieckiemu - a droga do Ojczyzny stanie, przed Wami otworem.

S. 431.

SOLDIERS OF POLAND!

Great danger is threatening you. You escaped Katyn and came away alive from the Bolshevik paradise. Until now you've been lucky...but you are now undesirable. Stalin doesn't like the united Polish formations and is striving to destroy your Fatherland. Your leaders in London have received instructions from Moscow to get rid of you by simple means.

33

For the time being you've remained in quite positions in a central section of the Italian frontier. You are now going to be thrown into the hell of Cassino. A few years ago, Stalin sent an army of murderers to get rid of your friends in Katyn. But the English are brighter. They are sending you to the Cassino front so that you may be killed in an aureole of heroism.

POLISH SOLDIERS!

Are you going to follow this game which you've been thrown into?

In this situation, you have only one means of salvation – come to us and you will live to see your Fatherland again. Protected by the German soldiers, who are sheltering Europe and Poland from the Bolsheviks, you will be able to work peacefully at your own will.

Two words

GO HOME!

will decide your future – life or death.

Tell this slogan to the first post on the German frontier, and the road to your Fatherland will be opened to you.

POLISH SOLDIERS!

ARE THESE THE COLORS OF YOUR COUNTRY?

NO!

This is a British flag! The English, under whose flag you are at present fighting, have betrayed you and given your Fatherland – Poland – to the Soviets.

CHURCHILL AND ROOSEVELT HAVE PUT POLAND INTO A SOVIET ALLIANCE.

Thanks to the British and Americans, you are deprived of your Fatherland!

POLSKI ŻOŁNIERZU!

Czyż są to barwy Twego kraju?

NIE!

To jest sztandar brytyjski! Anglicy, pod których sztandarem obecnie walczysz, zdradzili Twoją Ojczyznę, zdradzili Polskę na rzecz Sowietów.

CHURCHILL I ROOSEVELT PRZESZACHROWALI POLSKĘ ZWIĄZKOWI RADZIECKIEMU.

Anglikom i AMERYKANOM masz do zawdzięczenia, że stałeś się człowiekiem, pozbawionym Ojczyzny!

34

CZYŻ JEST TO SZTANDAR TWEGO KRAJU?

O, NIE!

To są barwy sowieckie. Zgodnie z życzeniem Anglików ma ona powiewać nad Twoją Ojczyzną. Pod czerwonym sztandarem z sierpem i młotem musiałeś służyć w Rosji sowieckiej.

BOLSZEWICY SPRZEDALI CIĘ WÓWCZAS ANGLIKOM.

Poprzez Iran, Palestynę i Egipt przywędrowałeś do Włoch, gdzie wymagają od Ciebie ofiary z krwi i życia dla dobra Angliji!

S 413

Leaflet 6 back

IS THIS YOUR COUNTRY'S FLAG?

DEFINITELY NOT!

These are Soviet Colors. In compliance with the wishes of the English, they are to fly over your Fatherland. You had to serve in Soviet Russia under the red flag with the sickle and hammer.

THE BOLSHEVIKS THEN SOLD YOU TO THE ENGLISH.

Having traveled through Iran, Palestine and Egypt, you've landed in Italy, where sacrifices of blood and life are required of you for England's benefit!

DO POLSKICH OFICERÓW I ŻOŁNIERZY!

Cały świat dowiedział się z uczuciem grozy o straszliwych bestialstwach, dokonanych przez najzawziętszego wroga Polski, krwawy bolszewizm, na narodzie polskim.

Z pośród oficerów Armji Polskiej, którzy w roku 1939 dostali się do niewoli sowieckiej, nikt prawie nie pozostał przy życiu. Bez różnicy: generał to był, czy podporucznik, wszyscy podzielili ten sam los w lesie pod Katyniem, w kwietniu 1940 roku: padli naskutek strzałów czerwonego komisarza w potylicę! Zbrodnię tą, popełnioną przez bestię reżimu sowieckiego, stwierdziła międzynarodowa komisja, a groza jej ukazała się w całej okropnej nagości oczom świata. 12.000 polskich oficerów, kwiat polskiej młodzieży, duma narodu polskiego legła wymordowana przez bandytów z Kremla, stanowiąc ofiarę czerwonego szaleństwa, dążącego do opanowania całego świata.

Ci sami bolszewicy, którzy zlikwidowali polskich oficerów, zamęczyli długimi i okropnymi katuszami prawie 3 miliony Polaków w tajgach Syberji, w obozach koncentracyjnych nad Morzem Północnym i w stepach Kazakstanu, każąc im umierać powoli, zdala od ziemi ojczystej.

A ty, polski oficerze i żołnierzu, chcesz oddawać swe życie za morderców twojego narodu, z którymi Anglia i Stany Zjednoczone zawarły sojusz, sprzedając bez skrupułów Twój kraj w ręce Stalina? **Czyniąc to, zdradzasz swój własny naród!**

Przechodź do nas! Nawet w piątym roku wojny masz zapewniony powrót do ojczyzny. Będziesz tam mógł lepiej i owocniej służyć narodowi!

S 408.

TO POLISH OFFICERS AND SOLDIERS!

The whole world learned with horror of the terrible bestialities bestowed on the Polish people by the blood-thirsty Bolsheviks.

Practically none of the Officers of the Polish Army, who in 1939 were imprisoned by the Soviets, survived. Whether General or Second Lieutenant – it made no difference – all shared the same fate in the forest at Katyn in April 1940. They fell, shot in the backs of their heads by the Red Commissar. This crime, committed by the bestial Soviet regime, was confirmed by the International Committee and the horror displayed to the whole world. 12,000 Polish Officers, the bloom of Polish youth, Poland's pride, were murdered by bandits from the Kremlin, victims of the madness of the Reds, aspiring to control the whole world.

These same Bolsheviks who got rid of Polish Officers, tortured, using long and atrocious methods, nearly 3 million Poles in Siberia, in concentration camps by the North Sea and the Kazakstan Steppes, telling them to die slowly, far from their Fatherland.

And you, Polish Officer and Soldier, want to give up your life for the murderers of your people who, together with England in a closed alliance, are, without scruples, selling your country to Stalin? **THINK ON IT, YOU'RE BETRAYING YOUR OWN COUNTRY!**

COME TO US! EVEN IN THE 5TH YEAR OF THE WAR, WE PROMISE YOU A RETURN TO YOUR FATHERLAND. THERE, YOU WILL BE ABLE TO SERVE YOUR NATIONALS.

POLISH FRIENDS!

38

DO YOU
WANT TO DIE
FOR THESE?

Kolego Polaku!

Ty walczysz, ale o przykrościach i udrękach wojny nie wiedzą nic ci, którzy ponoszą winę klęski Polski, którzy przyczyniają się do masowego wymierania narodów i do tych wszystkich potworności, jakie wniosły ze sobą 5 lat trwające zmagania. Wy musicie cierpieć dlatego, że oni prowadzą Waszym kosztem najbrudniejsze interesy.

I wojna trwa dalej ...

Najlepsze interesy robią na niej żydzi.

Wy tułacie się zdala od najbliższych, na dalekiej obczyźnie, Kanciarze i oszuści wojenni są zdala od frontu, korzystając z wszelkich wygód, otoczeni rodzinami. Ale Was pchają do walki, siedząc w cieple domowego ogniska, gdzie niczego im nie brak Kosztem waszego trudu i znoju żołnierskiego, kosztem waszej krwi, zbierają miljony i miljardy. Ich to nic nie obchodzi, że Wy giniecie! Bo dla nich najważniejsze są olbrzymie zyski.

Zarówno Wasze jak i nasze rodziny dotkliwie odczuwają piętno wojny, Muszą ciężko pracować i martwią się o Wasz los, o Wasze życie. Poznali oni czerwoną zarazę, nadciągającą ze wschodu.

Wasze rodziny nie wierzą, aby zwycięstwo Stalina mogło uszczęśliwić Polskę.

Czy pragnęlibyście dowiedzieć się, jak powodzi się Waszym najbliższym, co myślą o wojnie i z jaką tęsknotą na Was czekają ?

Jeśli tak – to przybądźcie do nas! Zapewniamy Wam natychmiastowy powrót do Ojczyzny, do Waszych domów rodzinnych.

Wasze żony, Wasze dzieci i Wasza ukochana Ojczyzna oczekują Was!

Hasło: Do domu !

S. 415.

DEAR POLISH FRIEND!

You are fighting, but those who are toasting to the defeat of Poland, who are contributing to the mass murder of a nation, do not know anything about the pains and anxieties of war, and do not appreciate the effect of 5 years' struggling. You are suffering because they are looking after their own dirty business at your cost.

And the war goes on...

THE JEWS ARE GETTING THE BEST OUT OF IT.

You are wandering far from your close ones, in a far-away country. The swindlers and impostors of the war are away from the front, enjoying every comfort, surrounded by their families. But they are pushing you to war whilst sitting in their warm homes where they do not want for anything. At the cost of your pains and toils, at the cost of your blood, they are collecting millions. They do not care that you are disappearing, because gigantic profits are more important to them.

Your families, like ours, are really feeling the effects of the war. They have to work hard, and they worry about your fate, about your life. They have recognised the red disease approaching from the East. Your families do not believe that Stalin's victory can make Poland happy.

Would you like to know how your nearest and dearest are, what they think of the war, and how they are yearning for you?

If you do – come to us. We assure you an instant return to your Fatherland.

Your wives, children and beloved Fatherland await you!

SLOGAN: GO HOME!

39

Italy, 21/4/1944

To Corporal Kluski, 2nd Company, 15th Battalion, 5th Brigade, 2nd Division.

My Dear Group Leader!
I have been on the German side since the 28th of March. I am living well and prospering, and am not being treated like a prisoner. On the evening of the 28th, both Szatkowski and I were on duty. We were taking turns, and it was Szatkowski's turn to sleep. I made up my mind to cross to the German side, which was no surprise, as I had always thought about this. When I was leaving, I went to the Corporal and took the password. As I was leaving my post, I watched my friend, Szatkowski for a long time, who was sleeping so well. I was sorry to leave a good friend, with whom I had lived like a brother. I do not know if you suspect me because I

opuszczać dobrego kolegę, z którym tak żyłem jak z bratem. Nie wiem jak posądzacie mnie, że zabrałem karabin maszynowy. Przepuszczam, że rozumiecie dla czego musiałem zabrać ze sobą – dla własnej obrony.–

W bliskich dniach pojadę do kraju, może Pan Bóg da, że zobaczę się z moją rodziną. Bo przepuszczam, że rodzina wyjechała gdzieś na zachód, gdyż tereny moje zajęte przez Bolszewików. Na tym kończę swój list.

Zasyłam jak najserdeczniejsze pozdrowienia panu Kapralowi Klusce, Szatkowskiemu i kolegom 15 tego bataljonu – rzeczywiście, kto mnie zna.–

"Czołem!

Siniuk Jan.

took a machine gun. I assume that you will understand why I took it – for protection.
In the next few days I shall go to my country. If God permits, I will see my family. I believe, however, that they have gone somewhere to the West as my country has been occupied by the Bolsheviks.
On this note, I'll finish.

41

I send my very best wishes to you Corporal Kluski, to Szatkowski and my friends of the 15th Battalion – and everybody who knows me.

Siniuk Jan

On active service

Pan Kap. Klusek

Polish Forces M.E. 312.

Written in Polish.

COLLEAGUES!

HAVE YOU HEARD WANDA?
"WANDA" BROADCASTS DAILY:

From 13.00 to 13.15 on short wave 28.3, 10,600 kilo hertz and 39,6, 7,575 kilohertz.

From 18.00 to 18.90 on medium wave 449,1 m, 668 kilohertz, or short wave 28,3 m, 10,600 kilo hertz, and 39,6 m, 7,575 kilohertz.

From 19.30 to 20.30 on all wave lengths as at 18.00

From 23.30 to 23.45 on medium and short wave, namely 420,8 m, 713 kilohertz, 31,4 m, 9,551 kilohertz, and also on all higher wave lengths.

"Wanda" has already helped some of your friends to go home. Corporal Stanislaw Borowski from the 3rd Carpathian Division, 2nd Brigade, 6th Battalion, 1st Company wrote to us from his home, a humane place. He's asked us to wish you all well on his behalf. His mother is alive, his family have survived the war. Corporal Borowski had a good journey, found everybody in good health and is spending Easter with them.

YOU MUST LISTEN TO "WANDA"!

Find a suitable opportunity and discuss the details. You shouldn't believe the stories you are hearing about the way the German soldiers are treating you. The Germans are decent soldiers and are guaranteeing you a return home. In Poland you'll have complete freedom in your choice of work – just give yourself up at the German battle front.

SO LISTEN TO "WANDA"!

You'll get to know what you want to know.

42

KOLEDZY!

Czy słyszeliście już Wandę?
„WANDA" mówi codziennie

od godz. 13.00 do 13.15 na falach krótkich 28.3 lub 10,600 Kilocyklów i 39,6 lub 7,575 Kilocyklów.

od godz. 18.00 do 18.90 na fali średniej 449,1 m lub 668 Kilocyklów oraz na falach krótkich 28,3 m lub 10,600 Kilocyklów, oraz 39,6 m lub 7,575 Kilocyklów,

od godz. 19.30 do 20.30 na wszystkich falach jak o godz. 18-ej,

od godz. 23.30 do 23.45 na falach średnich i krótkich, mianowicie 420,8 m lub 713 Kilocyklów, 31,4 m lub 9,551 Kilocyklów, tudzież na wszystkich wyżej wymienionych falach łącznie.

„Wanda" pomogła już kilku Waszym kolegom w wyjeździe do domu. Kapral Stanisław Borkowski z 3 Dywizji Karpackiej, 2 Brygady, 6 Bataljonu, 1 kompanji pisał do nas z rodzinnej miejscowości Sulejów w pow. piotrkowskim, województwa łódzkiego. Prosi on, byśmy Was w jego imieniu pozdrowili. Matka jego żyje, jego krewni szczęśliwie przetrwali okres wojenny. Kapral Borkowski również szczęśliwie odbył podróż, zastając wszystkich przy zdrowiu i spędzając z nimi święta Wielkiejnocy.

Koniecznie musicie słuchać „WANDY"!

Stwórzcie sobie odpowiednią sposobność a szczegóły omówcie w Waszym gronie. Nie powinniście wierzyć bajeczkom, które Wam opowiadają na temat traktowania Was przez Niemców, Niemcy są przyzwoitymi żołnierzami a jako żołnierze dają Wam pełną porękę Waszego powrotu do domów, a w Polsce będziecie mieli zupełną swobodę w wyborze pracy, skoro tylko udacie się do niemieckich linij bojowych.

Słuchajcie zatem „WANDY"!

Od niej dowiecie się wiele szczegółów, które zapewne chcielibyście się dowiedzieć.

S. 421

Wypełnić rubryki i przesłać do Wandy!
Pisać Wyraźnie!
Twój list odejdzie do Ojczyzny!

Jeden z Was zbierze te kartki w charakterze posłańca korespondencji do kraju. Następnie uda się w stronę niemieckich okopów i spotkawszy niemieckich żołnierzy, powita ich słowami „Do domu"! Oni przyjmą go chętnie. Niemieccy żołnierze są doskonale o wszystkiem poinformowani i czekają na Was.

Nazwisko: ....

Imię: ....

Stopień służbowy: ....

Ostatni wiadomy Ci adres Twoich najbliższych oraz nazwisko i imię odbiorcy: ....

....

....

....

....

....

....

....

To miejsce przeznaczone jest do napisania listu w 30 słowach. Napisz, co masz zakomunikować Rodzinie i podaj pytania, Wanda załatwi szybko i postara się o rychłą odpowiedź na Twój list.–

FILL IN AND SEND OFF TO WANDA!

WRITE LEGIBLY!

YOUR LETTER WILL REACH YOUR FATHERLAND!

One of you, in the capacity of a correspondence messenger, will collect these leaflets. He will then head for the German trenches and, on seeing the German soldiers, will greet them with the words "GO HOME!". They will readily welcome him. The Germans are well informed about everything and are awaiting you.

43

Surname:_____

Forenames:_____

Official Rank:_____

Last known address of your relations and name of

collector:_____

_____

_____

_____

_____

_____

_____

The space above is reserved for a letter of 30 words. Write what you want to say to your family and ask questions. Wanda will quickly organize matters and see that you receive an early reply to your letter.

44

Do domu!

Polscy żołnierze! Czy pomyśleliście nad tem, z kim walczycie wspólnie we Włoszech?

Anglicy potrafili zawsze radzić sobie i gdy sytuacja była poważna, gdy chodziło o ich skórę, starali się, aby inni za nich walczyli. Sprowadzili zatem Amerykanów, następnie Kanadyjczyków, Francuzów z obozu de Gaule'a, Marokańczyków i Hindusów.

A wreszcie po Hindusach przyszła kolej na Was! Was traktuje się gorzej niż kolorowe wojska kolonialne.

Wasze rodziny zostały zesłane na osiedlenie się w pozbawionych żywej duszy stepach afrykańskich, wyludnionych obszarach Australji i Indyj. Te pustkowia szukają rąk roboczych i dlatego tam osiedlają Wasze rodziny, pozbawione własnej ojczyzny. Wasze dzieci wychowuje się w szkołach Palestyny jako żer armatni, potrzebny Anglji, Ameryce i Sowietom.

A Wy Żołnierze Polscy macie nastawiać karki jako legjon cudzoziemski, podobnie jak kolorowe wojska kolonialne! Dla kogo?

Jako mieszkańcy Europy macie być wykorzystywani podobnie jak się dzieje z Hindusami. Przybądźcie do nas, a my odeślemy Was do domów rodzinnych. Szkoda bowiem głowy każdego z mieszkańców Europy, który polegnie na wojnie w której zwycięscami chcą być amerykańscy kapitaliści i moskiewscy kaci.

S. 427.

GO HOME!

Polish soldiers! Have you thought about who you are fighting with in Italy?

When the situation has become serious and their skin has been at stake, the English have always managed to get others to fight for them.
They brought in the Americans, then the Canadians, the French from de Gaule's camps, the Moroccans and the Hindus.

THEN AFTER THE HINDUS IT WAS YOUR TURN! YOU ARE BEING TREATED WORSE THAN THE COLORED COLONIAL ARMIES.

Your families have been sent to settlements in the deprived African Steppes, in the de-populated areas of Australia and India. These deserts need workers, and therefore your families have been sent there, deprived of their Fatherland. Your children are being brought up in Palestinian schools like gun fodder, need by the English, Americans and Russians.

AND YOU, POLISH SOLDIERS, ARE TO GIVE YOUR NECKS LIKE AN ALIEN LEGION, LIKE THE COLORED COLONIAL ARMIES! FOR WHOM?

You are European citizens, yet you are being abused like Hindus. Surrender to us and we will send you to your family homes. European citizens who rely on the war are wasting their lives, so that the victors of the war can be American capitalists and Moscow heretics.

45

46

One mouse is the head of the Elephant

Once upon a time when an elephant was sleeping, a mouse came up to him and saw him sleeping so soundly, that he tied the elephant with a chain. Since then the elephant had to remain a slave to the mouse. One day a cat came by, and wanted to eat up the mouse. The mouse ran to the elephant and asked for help. He promised the elephant that if he helped, the mouse would then set him free. The innocent elephant helped the mouse against the cat and then asked him to release his chains. The mouse laughed at the elephant and replied: "You don't deserve to be set free, you are not fit for it." After a few days the same cat came again and attacked the mouse. The mouse once again went to the elephant to ask for help. The elephant then replied: "You are dishonest, a big traitor and a deceiver! I won't help you. I'll try to break my own chains by myself. It is good for the cat to eat you." And that is exactly what happened – the cat ate the mouse and the elephant applied a bit of strength to break his own chains and was free.

This is your state! A big country like India is a slave to a small country like Britain. The Indian soldiers should be fighting for their freedom, which can only be achieved if England is destroyed. Now you are fighting only to be enslaved more!

A small rat is ruling the elephant

Once upon a time a little rat came up to an elephant and told him "let me get on your back, and I'll scratch it, I will make you feel better." As the rat got on the elephant's back and began to scratch, the elephant fell asleep because he enjoyed it so much. The rat then captured the elephant. When the elephant woke up the rat was there laughing at him. But when a cat comes to eat the rat, right away the rat runs to the captured elephant asking for help. The rat promises the elephant freedom if he will chase the cat away. The elephant is naive and listens to the rat. So in hope of being freed, he chases the cat away. But the rat just laughs at the elephant and does not let him go. The next time a cat comes, the same story repeats and the rat still does not free the elephant. Finally when another cat comes to eat the rat, the elephant refuses to help the rat because he knows not to trust him. The elephant says "I am big and strong and I can free myself, I don't need a little rat to free me." The cat eats the rat and the elephant goes free and lives happily.

This is a message to the big country of India that is being controlled by tiny Britain. Britain deceived India before in WWI, asking Indian troops to fight and promisng their freedom in exchange. India does not need to be freed by little Britain, it can free itself because it has the power and the strength to do so. The Indian youth should fight for the freedom of their country and not get involved in this war for Britain.

Leaflet 12 back

God does not change the state of any civilization unless and until the civilization thinks of changing the state itself!

Indians!

Do you have any idea what is going around in the world?! Every civilization is trying its hardest to fight for its freedom. In India everything possible is being done in order to achieve this freedom. At the same time Japanese and German representatives have already promised Subhash Chandra Bose that they will help India in its war for freedom!

Now free Indian army!

Under the leadership of Subhash Chandra Bose the Japanese army has entered India through Burma and at this moment the free Indian flag is waving in the premises of Manipur. This army will fight until the British army is completely destroyed. Thousands of Indian soldiers in the British troops are running and joining the Indian National army to fight for their freedom against the British. From one side this is what is happening: the Indian soldiers are going back to fight for their own freedom, and on the other side you are still here helping those who have enslaved you, and without thinking you are helping those who have kept you slaves for over 200 years! For the British army you are fighting against yourselves (in place of the British)! And why is this death your fate? Because you are still slaves of the British! Fighting for England will strengthen the chains of your slavery. Dying with dignity is better then a life without any respect! Right now foreign armies are ruling India and disrespecting the Indian people!

Think about it!
What should you be doing now?

Everyone, Everyday, listen to Hindustani news from 5 to 6 o' clock on both shortwave and medium wave.

48

خدا نے آج تک اُس قوم کی حالت نہیں بدلی ۔ نہ ہو جو خود خیال آپ اپنی حالت کے بدلنے کا:

ہندوستانیو!

تم کو کچھ خبر ہے کہ دنیا میں کیا ہو رہا ہے؟ ہر ایک قوم اپنی آزادی کیلئے سر توڑ کوشش کر رہی ہے ۔ ہندوستان کے اندر اس غلامی سے نجات پانے کی ہر ممکن کوشش جاری ہے ۔ اور سابق سی جاپانی اور جرمنی حکومتیں ہندوستان کے بڑے رہنما سبھاش چندر بوس سے وعدہ کر چکی ہیں کہ وہ ہندوستان کی اس جنگ آزادی میں پوری پوری مدد دینگی

اب آزاد ہندی فوج

ہند نیتا سبھاش چندر بوس کی رہنمائی میں جاپانیوں کے ساتھ مل کر برما کی سرحد سے ہندوستان کے اندر داخل ہو چکی ہیں اور اس وقت منی پور ریاست پر آزاد ہندوستانی جھنڈا لہرا رہا ہے ۔ یہ قوی فوج اس وقت تک اپنا خون بہائے گی جب تک کہ انگریز بالکل ہندوستان سے نیست و نا بود نہ ہو جائینگے ۔ ہزاروں کی تعداد میں ہندوستانی سپاہی انگریزی فوج سے بھاگ بھاگ کر ہندوستانی قوی فوج میں روزانہ بل رہے ہیں ۔ ایک طرف تو یہ ہو رہا ہے اور دوسری طرف تم بغیر کچھ سمجھے غیر قوم جس نے دو سو سال سے تمہیں غلام بنا رکھا ہے! اسکا سہارا بنے ہوئے ہو ۔ اور اپنے ملک سے دور دراز ناحق پر انگریزوں کے بدلے میں جانیں قربان کر رہے ہو ۔ آخر یہ بے مطلب موت تمہارے حصے میں کیوں ہے؟ کیونکہ تم ابھی تک غلام ہو +
انگریزوں کا ساتھ دینا اپنی غلامی کی زنجیروں کو اور بھی مضبوط کرنا ہے +
عزت کی موت بے عزتی کی زندگی سے بہتر ہے ۔ اس وقت ہندوستان میں غیر ملکی فوجیں ہندوستانیوں پر ظلم ڈھا رہی ہیں اور انکی بے عزتی کر رہی ہیں +

غور کرو!
کہ ایسے موقع پر تمہیں کیا کرنا چاہئے!

Khudá ne áj tak us qaum ka hálat náhin badli
Ná ho jis ko khiyál áp apni hálat ke badalne ká.

HINDUSTÁNIO!

Tum ko kuchh khabar hai kih dunyá men kyá ho ráhá hai? Har ek qaum apni ázádi ke lie sar tor koshish kar rahi hai. Hindustán ke andar is ghulami se niját páne ki har mumkin koshish jári hai. Aur sáth hi Jápáni aur Jermani hakumaten Hindustán ke bare rehnumá Subhas Chandra Bose se wádá kar chuki hain ki woh Hindustán ki is Jang-ázádi men puri puri madad dengi.

AB ÁZÁD HINDI FAUJ

Hind Netá Subhash Chandra Bose ki rehnumái men Jápánion ka sáth milkar Burmá ki sarhad se Hindustán ke andar dákhil ho chuki hain, aur iswaqt Manipore Riyasat par azad Hindustani jhandá lahrá ráhá hai. Yeh qaumi fauj uswaqt tak apná khun báháegi jab tak kih angrez Hindustan se bilkul nest-o-nábud na ho jáenge. Házáron ki tádád men Hindustani sipáhi angrezi fauj se bhág bhág kar Hindustáni Qaumi Fauj men rozána mil rahe hain. Ek taraf to yeh ho ráhá hai, dusri taraf tum baghair soche samjhe ghair qaum, jis ne do sau sál se tumhen ghulám báná rakhá hai uská sath de rahe ho, aur apne mulk se dur daraz fásele par angrezon ke badle men jánen qurban kar rahe ho. Akhir yeh be matlab maut tumháre hisse men kion hai? Kionkih tum abhi tak ghulám ho. Angezon ká sath dená apni ghulámi ki zanjiron ko aur bhi mazbut karná hai. Izzat ki maut bhi be-izzati ki zindagi se behtar hai. Is waqt Hindustán men ghair mulki faujen Hindustánion par zulam dha rahi hain aur unki be-izzati kar rahi hain.

GHAUR KARO!

KIH AISE MAUQE PAR TUMHEN KIYA KARNÁ CHÁHIE!

Rozáná shám ko 5 1/2 se 6 baje tak BHAI BAND Radio se Hindustáni men khabren sunie. 449,1 Medium wave, 28,3 aur 39,6 Short Wave.

Indische Soldaten, die sich mit diesem Flugblatt den deutschen Linien nähern, sind als Überläufer anständig zu behandeln, zu verpflegen und unter Bewachung zurückzuschaffen.

LwP. 116 / AI. 115.3 44

Leaflet 13 back

Boycott
foreign goods!

دُکھ بھری ۔ پُر مصائب ۔ اور قربانیوں سے بھرپور
یہ ہے مہاتما جی کی زندگی

اس کے ہزاروں ساتھیوں نے بھی اس کی طرح مصیبتوں کا سامنا کیا اور سیاسی جیل بھگتی
یہ ہے ان کی محبت اپنے دیس کے لیے۔ یہ سب کچھ وہ اپنے ہندوستانی بھائیوں کے لیے کر رہے ہیں ۔ تمہارے لیے ؟

ہاں ! انہارے لیے اور تمہارے بچوں کے لیے بھی

تاکہ کم سے کم وہ اپنی روزی کمانے کے لیے برطانوی فوج میں بھرتی ہونے پر مجبور نہ ہوں !
اور اپنی جان مفت میں غیر ملکوں میں غیر قوم کے فائدے کے لیے تمہاری طرح ضائع کرنے سے باز رہ
سکیں ۔ اگر تم اپنی جان برطانوی سامراج کے لیے کھو دیتے ہو تو ان کی تمام قربانیاں تمہارے لیے بیکار گئیں ۔

زندہ رہو !

اور ان کی قربانیوں کو ضائع مت جانے دو ! بلکہ ان سے فائدہ اٹھاؤ !
جو کچھ بھی کرتے ہو اس کو پہلے خوب سوچو !

DUKH BHARI, PUR BHARPUR MASAIB, AUR QURBANION SE
YIH HAI MAHATMA JI KI ZINDAGI

Uske hazaron sathion ne bhi uski tarah musibaton ka samna kiya aur siyasi jail bhugti — Yih hai unki muhabbat apne desh ke lie — yih sab kuchh woh apne Hindustani Bhaion ke lie kar rahe hain, Tumhare lie?

HAN TUMHARE LIE AUR TUMHARE BACHCHON KE LIE BHI

ta kih ham se kam woh apni rozi kamane ke lie Bartanwi fauj men bharti hone par majbur na hon. Aur apni jan muft men ghair mulkon men ghair qaum ke faide ke lie tamhari tarah zae karne se baz reh saken. Agar tum apni jan Bartanwi samraj ke lie kho dete ho to unki tamam qurbanian tumhare lie bekar gain

ZINDA RAHO!

Aur unki qurbanion ko zae mat jane do! Aur un se faeda uthao.

JO KUCHH BHI KARTE HO USKO PAHLE KHUB SOCHO!

△ 163 / 944

Full of sorrow, and plenty of problems and sacrifices is what Mahatmas' life is.

His thousands of companions also had to face the hardship of being a political prisoner. This is all for love for their country! They are doing all this for their country, for their Indian brothers, for you, **Yes for you! And your children too!**

51

So at least they shouldn't have to join the army to fulfill their hunger and earn a living – and they shouldn't have to give up their life for free for some other country and other race. Like you! And if you lose your life for this army all of the sacrifices of Mahatmas will go to waste.

Be alive!
Don't let the sacrifices be in vain!
Take advantage of that whatever you do!
Think really hard before doing anything!

52

SAFE CONDUCT

The soldier who carries this safe conduct is using it as a sign of his genuine wish to give himself up. He is to be disarmed, to be well looked after, to receive food and medical attention as required, and to be removed from the danger zone as soon as possible.

H.R. Alexander
FIELD MARSHAL

Translations in German, Italian and Polish on other side.

Supreme Allied Commander in the Mediterranean Theatre of Operations

SAFE CONDUCT

PASSIERSCHEIN
(wörtliche Uebersetzung des umstehenden Textes)

Der Soldat, der diesen Passierschein vorzeigt, benutzt ihn als Zeichen seines ehrlichen Willens, sich zu ergeben. **Er ist zu entwaffnen. Er muss gut behandelt werden. Er hat** Anspruch auf Verpflegung und, wenn nötig, ärztliche Behandlung. Er wird so bald wie möglich aus der Gefahrenzone entfernt.

GEZEICHNET
Oberbefehlshaber der Alliierten Armeen in Italien

SALVACONDOTTO
(Traduzione letterale del testo a tergo)

Il soldato che porta con se questo salvacondotto lo usa per dimostrare la sua sincera volontà di arrendersi. Bisogna disarmarlo, aver cura di lui, dargli da mangiare e prestargli, se necessario, assistenza medica. Al più presto possibile, egli deve essere allontanato dalla zona delle operazioni militari.

FIRMATO
Comandante Supremo delle Forze Alleate in Italia

PRZEPUSTKA
(Dokładne tłomaczenie tekstu na drugiej stronie)

Dla bojowych posterunków **SPRZYMIERZONYCH ARMII:** Żołnierz, okaziciel niniejszej przepustki, używa jej dla okazania swej szczerej woli do poddania się. Należy go rozbroić.

Powinien być dobrze traktówany. Przysługuje mu wyżywienie i w razie potrzeby opieka lekarska. Że strefy zagrożonej należy go bezzwłocznie usunąć.

PODPISANO
Naczelny Dowódca SPRZYMIERZONYCH ARMII we Włoszech

53

Leaflet 15 back

54

Where is Hitler?

Long live Himmler!

The distribution of German propaganda on May 11, 1944, was so heavy that the Allied High Commander felt it advisable, with a translation, to circulate an example of its own efforts. This spread shows a letter from a German girl to her soldier sweetheart. This is the German language version. The English version of this letter, with a transcription in English, follows on the next spread.

The preceding leaflets, 15 and 16, show other concepts of Allied Propaganda.

56

Leaflet 17 front

ganz zu schweigen von dem Mann von selbst. Was ich dir hier schreibe ist kein Märchen oder eine Lüge, sondern eine Tatsache, die ich selbst miterlebte. Kannst du mir sagen, ob das vielleicht von Charakter zeugt, wenn hochrangige Herren, nachdem mal eine Landeskriegsprobe an ihre Herrschaft sich gehen und Uniformen und Abzeichen und alle preußischen Zeichen vernichten? Dass die Führerbilder das nächste Vernichtungsobjekt sind, ist ebenfalls nur eine traurige Tatsache. So weit sind wir aber schon gekommen, dann kann man es den Soldaten an der Front, die schon 5 Jahren im Kampf stehen, bestimmt nicht verdenken, wenn sie ein baldiges Kriegsende herbeisehnen. Ich habe bisher noch jeden Menschen gesprochen, der seine Ideen und Anschauungen vertridigt, aber von jetzt nur von sein bißchen Leben denkt und gleich den Wunsch schwächt, das ist nur Lüge. Ich wünsche mir auch mal, ein bewußtes Glück in diesem Leben zu finden. Ein weiter Kampf wird es immer bleiben, und wofür? Unsere Zukunft ist so ungewiss, nirgend vor ein verschwindendes Ziel. Es küsst dich ganz dein

Ritter

Bonn, September 17th 1944

Dearest Paul,

This is going to be anything but a cheerful letter, I can tell you. Anyway, it's the last. What's going to happen is in the lap of the Gods. The front has come so terribly near. Paul, I wouldn't dream of writing to you like this just for fun: I only need to look at my luggage, all packed, and the word "war" comes like a blow to drive away any kind of excited sentimentality. We've come to a point, alas, when we must leave even Bonn — that little paradise, as it used to be, amongst so many shattered towns. Where are we going? This is the beginning of the great migration: people move along the high roads like tramps, loaded with their pitiful bundles. How many tears must be shed at leaving house and home. Is no mercy to be shown to us as human beings?

The last fortnight has been a nerve-shattering trial for us, and however we steel our wills we can't stave off anything. All I know is that the Führer needs men who are ready to live, and also to die, for their ideas. What's going on here is so contemptible and cowardly that I'm seething with rage! You can't imagine how the women are quaking with fear for their menfolk in the Party — not to speak of the men themselves! What sort of people are they? Can you tell me? — Party Members who, once they have been put to a little bit of testing, go off and destroy their uniforms and all documents?

The fact that the pictures of the Führer are the first things to be destroyed is just one additional sad fact. Things have come to such a pass that one can't think ill of the soldiers at the front, who've been in the war for five years, if they wish for a speedy end to it.

Until now I respected any man who defended his ideas and views, but a man who at this time simply clings to his little bit of life and at once becomes a turncoat — he's a scoundrel.

I wish merciful fate would put an end to this life. It will never be anything but fighting. And what for? Our future is so uncertain. Nothing anywhere is worth striving for.

Love and kisses,

Eternally yours

Rita.

The fact that the pictures of the Führer are the first things to be destroyed is just one additional sad fact. Things have come to such a pass that one can't think ill of the soldiers at the front, who've been in the war for two years, if they wish for a speedy end to it.

Until now I respected any man who defended his ideas and views, but a man who at this time simply clings to his little bit of life and at once becomes a turncoat — he's a scoundrel.

I wish merciful fate would put an end to this life. It will never be anything but fighting. And what for? Our future is so uncertain. Nothing anywhere is worth striving for.

Love and kisses,

Eternally yours,

Rita

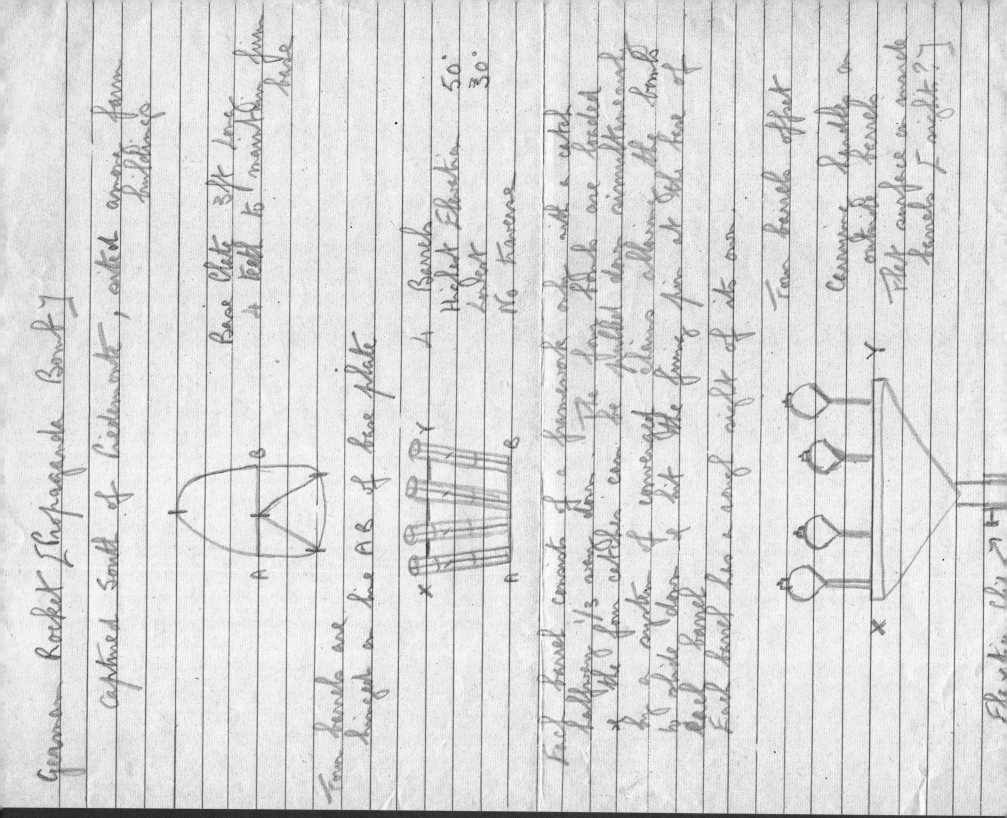

Sketches and notes made by Peter Batty during the Battle of Cassino showing the captured mortar launcher that had been used to scatter the propaganda leaflets featured in this book.

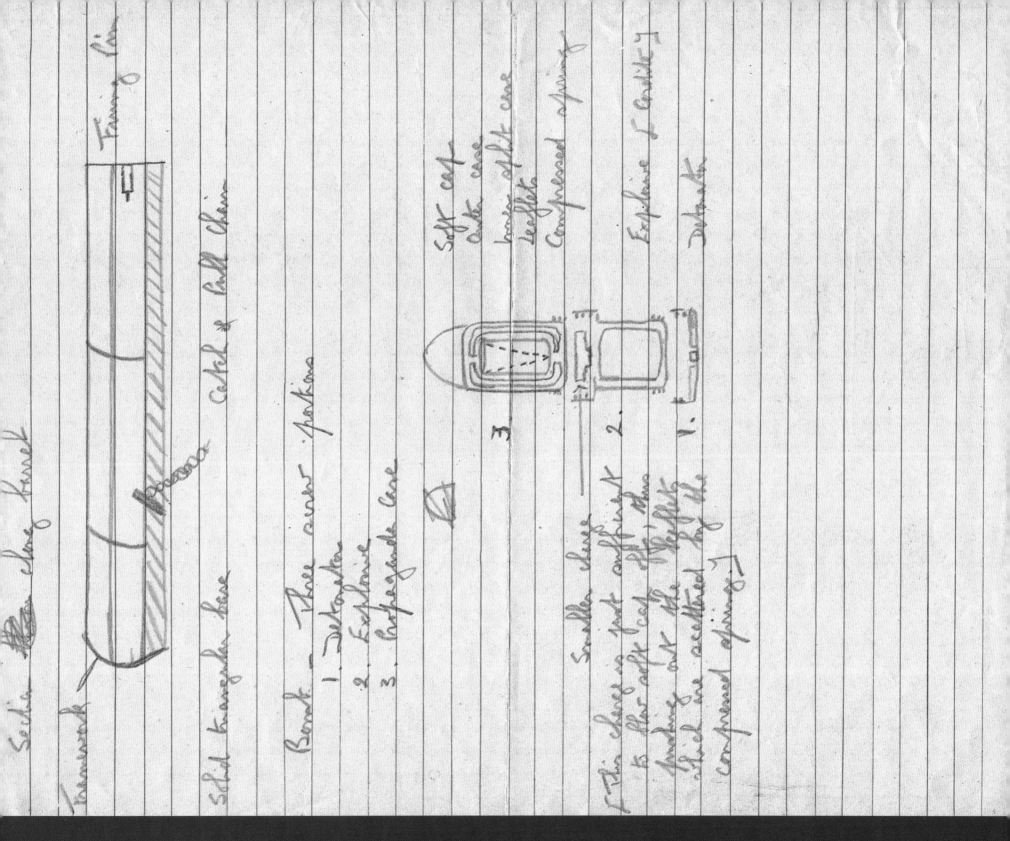

Excerpt from P.B.'s sketchbook, back

ALLIED FORCE HEADQUARTERS

2 May, 1945

SPECIAL ORDER OF THE DAY

Soldiers, Sailors and Airmen of the Allied Forces in the Mediterranean Theatre

After nearly two years of hard and continuous fighting which started in Sicily in the summer of 1943, you stand today as the victors of the Italian Campaign.

You have won a victory which has ended in the complete and utter rout of the German armed forces in the Mediterranean. By clearing Italy of the last Nazi aggressor, you have liberated a country of over 40,000,000 people.

Today the remnants of a once proud Army have laid down their arms to you—close on a million men with all their arms, equipment and impedimenta.

You may well be proud of this great and victorious campaign which will long live in history as one of the greatest and most successful ever waged.

No praise is high enough for you sailors, soldiers, airmen and workers of the United Forces in Italy for your magnificent triumph.

My gratitude to you and my admiration is unbounded and only equalled by the pride which is mine in being your Commander-in-Chief.

H. R. Alexander

Field-Marshal,
Supreme Allied Commander,
Mediterranean Theatre.

Afterword

Captain Peter Batty (1924 – 2004) was a liaison officer attached to the 8th Indian Division and took part in the action that occurred on May 11, 1944, and for the rest of the fourth battle of Monte Cassino. During the day leading up to the battle he collected the propaganda leaflets that the Germans fired at the Allied troops, and kept them safe since then. These leaflets, and his notes made during the battle, are the main content of this book.

Paper War
Nazi propaganda in one battle, on a single day
Cassino, Italy, May 11, 1944

Design and Production: Nicole Recchia

Our appreciation for Translations provided by Nandini Kotha,
Syed Khalid Ahmed, Randall L. Bytwerk, and Aktar Khan.

Words at War © Randall L. Bytwerk
Thursday, May 11, 1944 © Peter and Mark Batty
Map illustration on page 6 © Ryan Bruce
Photograph NA 15141 on page 13 © Crown Rights,
    courtesy of the Imperial War Museum

64

This book is typeset in Linotype Serifa and Frutiger.

Library of Congress Control Number:
2005921393

Printed and bound at the National Press
The Hashemite Kingdom of Jordan

10 9 8 7 6 5 4 3 2 1   First Edition

This edition © 2005
Mark Batty Publisher
6050 Boulevard East, Suite 2H
West New York, NJ 07093

www.markbattypublisher.com

ISBN: 0-9762245-0-X